Who Was
Nelson Mandela?

by Pam Pollack and Meg Belviso
illustrated by Stephen Marchesi

Grosset & Dunlap
An Imprint of Penguin Random House

59811

For Joanne Barkan, who stayed up in New York City
to see Madiba walk out of jail—PP

To Joan S. Belviso, Umama and Makhulu—MB

For Doug Jetta, Ricardo Gittings, and Medrano McPherson,
who taught me by example—SM

GROSSET & DUNLAP
Penguin Young Readers Group
An Imprint of Penguin Random House LLC

Text copyright © 2014 by Pam Pollack and Meg Belviso. Illustrations copyright © 2014 by Stephen Marchesi. Cover illustration copyright © 2014 by Penguin Random House LLC. All rights reserved. Published by Grosset & Dunlap, an imprint of Penguin Random House LLC, 345 Hudson Street, New York, New York 10014. The WHO HQ™ colophon and GROSSET & DUNLAP are trademarks of Penguin Random House LLC. Printed in the USA.

Library of Congress Control Number: 2013032706

ISBN 978-0-448-47933-0   15 14 13 12 11 10 9 8

Who Was
Nelson Mandela?

Contents

Who Was
Nelson Mandela?

In the heart of Thembuland, in South Africa, was a grand house. The local people called it "the Great Place." Here lived Jongintaba, who ruled as king. The Great Place was his royal home.

On this day in 1927, Jongintaba was holding a tribal meeting. The men talked about important matters. Also in the room was a young boy who had come to live at the Great Place only a short time before. He was nine years old. After the boy's own father died, the king had adopted him.

The boy listened to the men talk and watched his foster father. The king did not speak. He listened. He thought everyone deserved a voice in his kingdom, no matter who they were. Then, when he sensed that people had said all they needed to, the king gave his opinion. This approach was very different from the way the rest of the country of South Africa was ruled.

South Africa is a country at the bottom tip of the African continent. It is almost twice the size of Texas. Once black kings had ruled South Africa. Then white settlers came from Europe. They grabbed land for themselves and took control of the country. By the late 1800s, black South

Africans had no voice in the government. By the
time the boy came to live with his new foster
father, there were about six million people in
South Africa—and about four million were black.
And yet they weren't truly citizens of their own
country. They couldn't vote. They could only live
where the government allowed them to live. Even
kings like Jongintaba had no real power.

As the nine-year-old watched his foster father's meeting, he dreamed of a different South Africa, one where people of all colors had a voice. Where everyone was free and equal. When he grew up he hoped to make that happen.

The boy's name was Nelson Mandela. One day he would change South Africa. One day he would change the world.

Chapter 1
Troublemaker

The boy's name had been Rolihlahla (Roh-lee-LAH-lah). In his native language, the word meant *tree shaker*. But it also meant *troublemaker*. The boy's father was chief of the people called the Thembu tribe. Like many chiefs, he had more than one wife, and he also had thirteen children. The boy's mother, Nosekeni Fanny, was her husband's third wife. Rolihlahla was the first of his mother's four children. He was born on July 18, 1918.

At the time, South Africa was ruled by the
British. The white government strictly controlled
what black South Africans did and where they
went. Black people had to stay in their own
neighborhoods and villages, which were called
homelands. If a black person left his homeland
for any reason, he had to carry a special pass that
gave him permission to travel, even if he was only

going to a white neighborhood to work for the day. A black person without a good reason for being in a white neighborhood would be arrested.

When Rolihlahla's father ignored a summons from the British government to appear in court, he was stripped of his title and most of his land and cattle. The boy and his mother went to live in the village where she'd been born. The boy went to a school run by Christian missionaries from Europe. For his first day of school his father had given him a pair of his own trousers cut off at the knee to replace the blanket dyed in red clay

he wore at home. When the boy got to school his
teacher gave him something else: a Western name.
From that day on, Rolihlahla would be called
Nelson. Nelson Mandela.

Nelson shared three small huts with his mother
and younger sisters. He brought sheep and calves
to and from the pasture. His favorite game was
stick fighting—a traditional South African sport
that is a bit like sword fighting. Players hold
two sticks, one in each hand. They try to strike

while blocking at the same time. Nelson was a champion in his village.

It was always a special time when his father visited the family. However, during one of his visits home, Nelson's father became sick and died. Not only was his father gone, but Nelson would no longer live in the village with his sisters and mother. He was going to have a new foster father: Jongintaba.

Nelson and his mother walked west from the village carrying all of Nelson's belongings. They

walked all day on rocky roads. When they arrived,
Nelson couldn't believe his eyes. He had never
seen a home as big as this one. A fancy car drove
through the open gate. The man who stepped out
was short and heavy and wore a European-style
suit. This was Jongintaba.

Although Nelson's new world intrigued him,
it was scary being in a strange place all alone.
Luckily Jongintaba had a son named Justice,

who was four years older than Nelson. The boys
hunted with slings, explored the countryside,
and raced horses. Nelson went to a better school
than he had in the village. He studied English,
history, and geography. But he learned the most
by going to meetings with the tribal elders. Nelson
dreamed that one day he might be a great leader
like his foster father.

Nelson loved to listen to stories of African

THE EUROPEANS ARRIVE

IN THE FIFTEENTH CENTURY, EUROPEAN NATIONS
WERE SENDING GREAT SHIPS ALL OVER THE
WORLD. THE EASTBOUND SHIPS THAT WERE
HEADED FOR ASIA USUALLY PASSED AROUND THE
BOTTOM TIP OF THE AFRICAN CONTINENT. THEY
STOPPED IN WHAT IS NOW KNOWN AS SOUTH
AFRICA TO RESTOCK FOOD AND WATER. IN 1647
A DUTCH SHIP WRECKED ON THE SOUTHWEST
COAST. THE SURVIVING SAILORS LIKED THE AREA
SO MUCH, THEY STAYED AND BUILT A FORT. SO
MANY DUTCH CAME AS SETTLERS, THEY PUSHED

THE NATIVE PEOPLE OFF THEIR LANDS. THE DUTCH
FORMED THEIR OWN COLONY, A COMMUNITY
IN AFRICA UNDER DUTCH RULE. THEN THE
EUROPEANS DISCOVERED GOLD AND DIAMONDS
IN SOUTH AFRICA. THAT MADE THE LAND EVEN
MORE VALUABLE. IN THE EIGHTEENTH CENTURY
THE BRITISH TOOK OVER. MANY DUTCH SETTLERS
PUSHED FARTHER INTO AFRICAN LANDS TO GET
AWAY FROM THE BRITISH. IN 1902, AFTER THE
BRITISH AND DUTCH FOUGHT, SOUTH AFRICA'S
COLONIES BELONGED TO THE BRITISH.

heroes of the past, the men who fought against the Dutch and the British. In these stories black South Africans were ruled by their own kings like Jongintaba. "When the Europeans came to Africa," the tribal elders said, "they had the Bible and we had the land. They said, 'Let us pray.' We closed our eyes. When we opened them, we had the Bible and they had the land."

Chapter 2
City of Light

When Nelson was sixteen, he and Justice took part in an important ceremony where they became men in the eyes of the village. After the ceremony a tribal leader made a speech. "Among these young men are chiefs who will never rule because we have no power to govern ourselves," the man said.

Governing was exactly what Nelson wanted to do when he grew up. He attended a boarding school in Engcobo so that he could one day advise rulers like Jongintaba. Then in 1937 he transferred to Healdtown, a church-run college. From there he went to Fort Hare, the only all-black college in the country. Many white South Africans thought

FORT HARE

NATIVE AFFAIRS DEPARTMENT

that all black people needed to learn was how to
serve white people. Schools like Fort Hare gave
black South Africans bad ideas, they thought.
They made black people think they were as smart
as white people and could compete with them
for jobs.

Fort Hare did give Nelson ideas. He began
to study the world outside South Africa. Nelson
planned to one day work for the Native Affairs
Department, which enforced laws such as the "pass
laws" requiring all black South Africans to carry
a passport all the time. He hoped to change the

laws so that black people would be treated better.
He worked hard in school to reach his goals.

But in 1940 Nelson resigned from the

Students' Representative Council
in protest of the bad conditions
in the dorms. "Supper was
four remarkably thin slices of
bread," Nelson's college friend
Oliver Tambo would later say,
"taken with a small cup of milk water." The school
authorities said any student resigning from student
government would be expelled from school.
When Jongintaba found out that
Nelson had left school
he ordered him
to return.

He also
ordered
him to get
married.

He had found Nelson the perfect bride. She was "fat and dignified," Nelson said later. Some say she was in love with Justice.

Neither boy wanted to get married yet. So they ran away to the greatest city in South Africa. To Nelson Mandela, Johannesburg looked like a city of light. "A vast landscape of electricity," he called it.

He and Justice got jobs, but were soon caught by Jongintaba's men. Justice had to return home to take his father's place one day. But Nelson convinced his foster father to let him stay in the city and study law.

In Johannesburg, Nelson made new friends like Walter Sisulu. Sisulu was the son of a black cleaning lady and a white government official.

He had worked many different jobs and led strikes
for better wages for black workers. Sisulu got
Nelson a job at a law firm. He also encouraged
Nelson to enroll at a local university as a law
student. Nelson married Sisulu's cousin Evelyn in
1944, and they soon had a son, Thembi.

That same year Nelson joined the African
National Congress. The word *congress* did not
mean it was part of the government. It referred
to a group of many people all working for the
rights of black South Africans. When it was first
founded in 1912 the ANC led protests against the
pass laws. But by the late 1930s it had become
powerless. Nelson and his friends started a new
group within the ANC called the Youth League.
The Youth League led the ANC to challenge the
government. For the first time the ANC openly
accused white South Africans of not

having the best interests of black
South Africans at heart.
Nelson became so wrapped
up in the struggle he
hardly ever saw his young
family.

It was hard to imagine
the white government in

South Africa getting any worse for black people. But in 1948, it did. The government of South Africa started a cruel system of segregation, a way of keeping people of different races apart. In English the word for this system meant "apartness." In Afrikaans, the language of Dutch South Africans, it was called *apartheid*.

Chapter 3
Apartheid

Most white people in South Africa were descended from either British or Dutch settlers. The Dutch South Africans were called Afrikaners. They formed their own political party, the National Party, also called "the Nats." In 1948, when Nelson was twenty-nine years old, the Nats won control of the government by a slim margin.

The Nats believed black people were inferior

to whites. According to the Nats' laws of apartheid, everyone had to be labeled by their race: white, black, colored (people who were mixed race), and Indians (South Asians who had come to South Africa from India). If there was any doubt as to a person's race, tests were given, like having a pencil poked into their hair. If the pencil stuck, they were colored and not white. Marriage between races became illegal. Buses and schools were separated by race. Many of these laws already

reflected the way people were living, but once they became official law, it was going to be much harder for anything to change for black South Africans.

Most black South Africans lived outside city borders in neighborhoods called townships.

The townships were crowded. The houses were
often simple shacks with no electricity or indoor
plumbing. Black workers left the townships to
work for white people in the city during the day,
and then were forced to return to the townships
at night.

SEGREGATION IN THE UNITED STATES

JIM CROW LAWS WERE ENFORCED IN MUCH OF THE AMERICAN SOUTH FROM 1877 TO THE MID-1960S. THESE LOCAL AND STATE LAWS KEPT BLACK PEOPLE AND WHITE PEOPLE SEPARATE. IN MANY WAYS, THESE LAWS WERE NOT SO DIFFERENT FROM APARTHEID. UNDER JIM CROW LAWS, BLACK AMERICANS COULD NOT SIT ON BENCHES RESERVED FOR WHITE PEOPLE, ATTEND WHITE SCHOOLS, OR EVEN DRINK FROM WHITE WATER FOUNTAINS. ALSO, BLACK PEOPLE WERE EXPECTED TO ACT A CERTAIN WAY AROUND WHITE PEOPLE. A BLACK PERSON WAS FORBIDDEN FROM SHAKING HANDS WITH A WHITE PERSON. BLACK PEOPLE HAD TO ADDRESS WHITES FORMALLY, EITHER "MISTER" AND "MISS" OR "SIR" AND "MA'AM," WHILE WHITE PEOPLE CALLED BLACKS ONLY BY THEIR FIRST NAMES. ON THE ROAD, WHITE DRIVERS EVEN HAD THE RIGHT-OF-WAY AT ALL INTERSECTIONS!

When Nelson Mandela and his friends learned that the Nats had won the election, they were stunned. For years the Nats

had preached about the "*swart gevaar*," or "black danger," and white superiority. Nelson realized he could never work within the government as he had hoped. He and the rest of the Youth League would have to fight back through protests and acts of civil disobedience. Civil disobedience means peacefully breaking laws to show that the laws are unfair. In 1950 the white government made all protests, peaceful or not, illegal.

Nelson was becoming known as a protest leader—in other words, a troublemaker. He was living up to the name he'd been born with, Tree Shaker. He and Oliver Tambo, whom he had first met at Fort Hare, opened a black law firm—the first in Johannesburg—and they represented poor black defendants in court. Their clients were accused of all sorts of crimes. It was a crime to walk through a door marked for white people. It was a crime to be unemployed and a crime to be employed at the wrong place. Nelson also represented people who had been evicted from their homes because their neighborhoods had been declared white areas.

Nelson was a powerful figure in the courtroom, arguing for civil rights. He had a natural authority. But as he spent more and more time fighting for his clients, he saw less and less of his family. When he came to the hospital to see his newborn son, Makgatho, his five-year-old son, Thembi, asked, "Where does Daddy live?"

Chapter 4
The Defiance Campaign

In 1950, Nelson was elected president of the Youth League. In 1952 the ANC sent a letter to the prime minister saying that since all the ANC complaints had fallen on deaf ears, they were going to take action. Unless the government repealed—or struck down—the laws of apartheid by February 29, there would be a campaign of defiance. In other words, black people would refuse to obey the apartheid laws.

This time the ANC's complaints were not ignored. They were rejected. The government warned that anyone breaking the law would be severely punished. They might be arrested or forced to pay a big fine. Some people were beaten. Nelson led the protest anyway, raising funds

and rounding up volunteers to break the laws of
apartheid peacefully. For example, some were to

sit on whites-only benches or stand in whites-only lines. Nelson traveled all around the province speaking to workers and villagers, encouraging them to fight for their rights. They came to respect the man they called Mandela.

The Defiance Campaign, as this protest was called, would be peaceful. No matter what the government did to them, the protesters would not react with violence. They might be hurt, Mandela warned, but they must control their anger and fear. If they attacked, the government would easily crush them.

It was illegal to encourage anyone to break apartheid laws. However, Nelson and other ANC members recruited over 8,500 volunteers. Many wore armbands in green, gold, and black, the colors of the ANC: green for the land, gold for its riches, and black for the people.

PASSIVE RESISTANCE

"PASSIVE RESISTANCE" IS WHEN PEOPLE PEACEFULLY BREAK UNFAIR LAWS. THE AIM OF PASSIVE RESISTANCE IS TO END INJUSTICE BY REFUSING TO OBEY UNJUST LAWS. IT WAS EFFECTIVELY USED BY INDIAN LEADER MAHATMA GANDHI IN HIS STRUGGLE FOR INDIAN INDEPENDENCE FROM THE BRITISH IN THE 1920S, 1930S, AND 1940S. IT WAS ALSO USED IN THE

MAHATMA GANDHI

MARTIN LUTHER KING JR.

1950S AND 1960S BY CIVIL RIGHTS LEADERS IN THE US LIKE DR. MARTIN LUTHER KING JR. TO WIN EQUALITY FOR BLACKS. FOR EXAMPLE, CIVIL RIGHTS ACTIVISTS WOULD SIT AT LUNCH COUNTERS THAT WERE FOR WHITES ONLY. THEY'D SIT EVEN THOUGH NO ONE WOULD SERVE THEM. THEY'D SIT UNTIL POLICE CAME AND DRAGGED THEM AWAY, SOMETIMES TO JAIL. PEACEFUL RESISTANCE CAN BE A VERY POWERFUL WAY TO CHANGE UNJUST LAWS. THE SIGHT OF PEOPLE BEING ARRESTED AND ATTACKED JUST BECAUSE THEY WANT EQUALITY CAN TURN PUBLIC OPINION IN THEIR FAVOR.

Other countries took notice and admired the courage of the protesters. But the South African government cracked down hard on them. People were arrested and sometimes beaten. The police raided houses and arrested black leaders. As for Nelson Mandela, he was now forbidden to join any group, or write anything for a newspaper or magazine. He couldn't go to an airport or a school, or even leave his neighborhood in Johannesburg.

The Defiance Campaign was crushed. But thousands of new members had joined the ANC. Black citizens had seen that they could stand together against the white government. They had also seen how far the government was willing to go to stop them. They now understood that they might have to die to get equal rights. For many black South Africans, it was a sacrifice they were willing to make.

In 1953 the Nats were reelected. They outlawed missionary schools like the one young Nelson had attended, because these schools taught

black children the same way that white children were taught—in other words, they treated them like equals. The government passed an education act: All black children would be taught that they were inferior to whites and only good for serving them. A black child was taught just enough to become a janitor or house worker.

In 1955 the ANC called for a Congress of the People to agree on a bill of rights for all South

Africans, no matter what race. Nelson's friend Walter Sisulu helped organize the meeting. There were more than three thousand delegates from all over South Africa who gathered on June 25 and 26 on a soccer field outside Johannesburg. People traveled miles to be there. They sat on blankets in the grass. People of all races held banners saying "Freedom of Speech" or "We Want Better." On a platform in front of the crowd was a wheel with

COPE

CONGRESS
OF THE PEOPLE

four spokes symbolizing unity. The four spokes represented the main anti-apartheid political groups, with the ANC represented by the hub of the wheel in the center.

The bill of rights was called the Freedom Charter. The charter was read aloud in English and in two African languages, Xhosa and Sesotho. Each point was debated, just like in the tribal meetings of Nelson's childhood. The mood was joyous until the arrival of police with guns. The police grabbed the microphone and forbade anyone to leave. They arrested the leadership of the ANC including Oliver Tambo, Walter Sisulu, and Nelson Mandela.

The men were accused of treason. If found guilty, they could be put to death.

Chapter 5
Sharpeville

TREASON TRIAL

The ACCUSED

DECEMBER 1956

Nelson and his fellow defendants did not have to live in jail during the trial. They were let out on bail. They had to pay the government money as a promise they wouldn't escape to another country. When Nelson went home he found an empty house. His wife, Evelyn, had left and wanted a divorce. Nelson later said, "I could not give up my life in the struggle, and she could not live with my devotion to something other than herself and the family." They were divorced in 1958.

The "Treason Trial," as it came to be called, lasted from 1956 to 1961. When Nelson wasn't at court he threw himself into his law practice with Oliver Tambo. Tambo's charges were unexpectedly dropped after the first year, so he had more freedom to help black South Africans accused of crimes. As the months went by,

charges were dropped against more of the defendants. By 1959 only thirty of the 156 defendants were still facing charges in this trial, including Nelson.

One day during the trial Nelson glimpsed a woman waiting for a bus. She was beautiful. He longed to see her again, but he had no idea who she was. Some weeks later, the same woman arrived at his office. She had come with her brother to ask for legal help.

Her name was Nomzamo Winifred Madikizela—Winnie for short. Her name meant "she who strives." She was one of the first black hospital social workers in South Africa. Nelson asked her out for Indian food. Unlike Nelson's ex-wife Evelyn, Winnie was passionate about the ANC and politics. After that very first date, he proposed to Winnie. And she said yes! They were married on June 14, 1958. Winnie loved to watch her husband making speeches or arguing for civil rights. She attended protests and was arrested. She and Nelson had a baby girl, Zenani (called Zeni), in 1959.

Meanwhile, the ANC was changing. Nelson dreamed of a South Africa where white and black people lived together as friends. He thought the ANC should reach out to white citizens who were against apartheid. But many in the ANC did not want to work with white people. They didn't trust white South Africans. They did not

ROBERT SOBUKWE

want to compromise with the white apartheid government. In 1959 a civil rights leader, Robert Sobukwe, left the ANC. He founded PAC, the Pan Africanist Congress. Its slogan was "Our Land."

In March 1960, PAC asked blacks without their passbooks to approach policemen and get arrested on purpose. They hoped the jails would get so full that the government would

PAN AFRICANIST CONGRESS

have no choice but to get rid of the laws. Nelson thought this approach would put people in danger without doing much good.

Most people who participated in PAC's campaign were arrested without violence. But not those in the town of Sharpeville, about fifty miles from Johannesburg. On March 21, 1960, the black people of Sharpeville gathered to protest the pass laws. Police said the crowd numbered

twenty thousand. Others said it was more like five thousand. Eyewitnesses said the crowd was calm. They certainly had no guns or other weapons. Police said the people were armed with sticks and rocks. More police officers arrived to back up the Sharpeville officers, bringing the total of armed law-enforcement officers to three hundred.

The police tried to arrest the PAC leaders. The crowd pushed forward. The police pushed them back. Then two gunshots rang out. Those shots were followed by forty seconds of gunfire. The police fired more than seven hundred bullets into the crowd. People screamed and ran. Children threw their arms over their heads to protect

themselves. By the time the shooting stopped, sixty-nine people lay dead or dying, and another 180 were wounded seriously, including thirty-one women and nineteen children. Most of the dead were shot in the back in their attempt to escape the police. None of the policemen was seriously hurt.

A member of the white South African government called the incident an "ordinary police action." The rest of the world called it a massacre.

Chapter 6
Underground

Pictures of Sharpeville spread around the world. This was what apartheid looked like. Outside South Africa the killings were condemned. The United Nations blamed the South African government for what

happened. Foreign businesses pulled their investment money out of South Africa.

The government declared a state of emergency. Now the police could arrest anyone suspected of acting against the government—no proof needed. All public meetings were now illegal.

Sharpeville had a big effect on Nelson and the rest of the ANC. Nelson and Oliver Tambo had spoken in 1959 about what they should do in the event of a crisis like this. They thought one of them should leave South Africa to gain support for their cause around the world. But strong ANC leaders were also needed at home. They decided that Tambo should be the one to leave South Africa. Nelson would stay.

The next day police arrived at the Mandelas' door. In front of a pregnant Winnie and little Zenani, Nelson was arrested.

He stayed in jail for five months without being
charged with a crime. His second daughter,
Zindziswa (called Zindzi), was born in December
1960. Eventually, he was accused of the most
serious crime possible—trying to overthrow the
government.

On March 29, 1961, one year after the terrible Sharpeville murders, Nelson Mandela and the other defendants from the Treason Trial were finally found not guilty. The main judge on the three-judge panel said that although they had broken the law, he could find no proof that they were trying to overthrow the government.

During that same month, a civil-rights conference was held in Pietermaritzburg, South Africa. Nelson now planned to go underground. Leaving his family, he hid out with friends, slept during the day, and went out only at night. He met secretly with reporters. In interviews, he explained that Sharpeville had changed the way he thought about protest. He said, "In my mind, we are closing a chapter on this question of a nonviolent policy." Black South Africans had tried nonviolence to end apartheid. But events like Sharpeville showed that it didn't work. The South African government had no problem killing

peaceful protesters. Nelson and the ANC changed tactics. There was a need for armed resistance, so a new group was formed. It was called *Umkhonto we Sizwe* (oom-KOHN-toh-way-SEEZ-way), or Spear of the Nation. Nelson was its commander in chief. Although the new group did not want to kill people, it was ready to destroy power plants, railways, and telephone lines. By disrupting the running of the country, the Spear hoped to force the white government to end apartheid.

Nelson hid out on the Liliesleaf Farm in Rivonia with other ANC leaders like Walter Sisulu. To avoid arrest, he wore disguises. One day he was an errand boy, the next a chef. He dressed in the dusty overalls of a gardener or the beads and painted face of a tribal healer. He had many narrow escapes. One time he was spotted by a black guard— but the man simply gave him the ANC "thumbs-up" signal and turned the other

way. Whoever the guard was, he wanted Nelson to stay free. The government hated Nelson for outsmarting them.

Then Nelson's luck ran out. On August 5, 1962, the police stopped a car. In the passenger seat was a black man dressed as a chauffeur. It was Nelson. He tried to convince the policemen that his name was David Motsamayi. But the police didn't believe it. He was arrested.

Somehow the police had known that Nelson's car was going to come through that spot on that day. No one knows who betrayed him. Nelson was sentenced to five years in prison with hard labor. As the police took him away the crowd shouted, "*Tshotsholoza*, Mandela!" ("Struggle on, Mandela!")

Chapter 7
Robben Island

While Nelson was in prison, the police searched Liliesleaf and arrested Walter Sisulu and other members of Spear of the Nation. Luckily Oliver Tambo was outside South Africa. When he heard about the arrests he knew he couldn't go back. He was as determined as ever to help his friends.

In October 1963, Nelson went on trial again. He was accused of 222 acts of sabotage between 1961 and 1963. *Sabotage* means to destroy or disrupt things so that they don't work. For instance, Spear had plans to set off explosions in police stations and other government buildings (but not when people were around). The state asked for the maximum penalty: death by hanging.

The courtroom was tense. The lawyers against
Nelson and his friends took five months to present

their argument. Then, in April, Nelson stood to speak. His elderly mother and his wife watched from the gallery. He offered no evidence in his defense. Instead, he made a statement. "We believe that South Africa belongs to all the people who live in it," he said, "and not to one group, be it black or white."

Nelson spoke about the unjust laws, life in the crowded townships, and the cruel actions of the government. He spoke on the right to vote, the right to an education, and the right to be treated with basic respect. For hours the courtroom listened, spellbound. "I have dedicated myself to this struggle of the African people . . . ," Nelson said. "It is an ideal which I hope to live for and to achieve. But if needs be, it is an ideal for which I am prepared to die."

After the trial, the judge sentenced Nelson and the other defendants, including Walter Sisulu, to life in prison.

Nelson and Sisulu were flown to a maximum-security prison on Robben Island off the coast of Cape Town. No ships were allowed within a mile of the island. Escape was impossible. Mandela was led to the cell that would be his home for the next eighteen years. It was eight feet wide and seven feet long, lit by a single forty-watt lightbulb. The

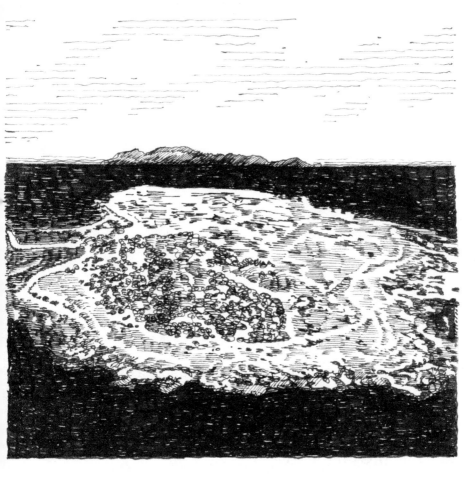

bulb stayed on day and night. Mandela could walk across the room in three steps. There was a mat for sleeping and three blankets so thin he could see through them. His toilet was a small iron bucket.

All the prisoners on Robben Island were black. All the guards were white. Mandela could write to his family and receive a letter from them only once every six months. Before Nelson was allowed to read a letter, prison officials crossed out anything in the letter they didn't think Nelson should see. Often so many words were crossed out, the letter barely made

sense. Nelson did not see Winnie for years at a time. He was not allowed to attend the funerals of his mother or his eldest son, Thembi, who died in a car accident in 1969.

Every day, he was woken up at five thirty. He washed and shaved with cold water. He emptied his iron bucket. He was allowed eight squares of toilet paper a day. He ate tasteless porridge for breakfast. Then he went to work—either breaking rocks in the courtyard or working in the limestone quarry digging out heavy slabs of rock with picks and shovels and lifting them onto

trucks. The sun was so bright on the limestone it damaged his eyesight. In the summer it was boiling hot; in winter, cold and windy. The lime dust stung his eyes and made his hands blister.

Information about the outside world came from new prisoners, except when guards left newspaper clippings on his sleeping mat to let him know that—back in Johannesburg—Winnie was being harassed and jailed. They did this to show Nelson how powerless he was to help his family.

WINNIE MANDELA

WINNIE MANDELA SHARED HER HUSBAND'S COMMITMENT TO ENDING APARTHEID. DURING THE YEARS NELSON SPENT IN PRISON, WINNIE WAS OFTEN JAILED, BEATEN, AND HARASSED. THIS TREATMENT LEFT HER ANGRY AND MADE HER SEE VIOLENCE AS AN ACCEPTABLE WAY OF DEALING WITH ENEMIES. SHE WAS PUT ON TRIAL FOR KIDNAPPING AND MURDER. MANY PEOPLE DIDN'T APPROVE OF HER AGGRESSIVE STYLE, BUT SHE REMAINED A WELL-KNOWN, IF CONTROVERSIAL, PUBLIC FIGURE. ALTHOUGH SOME PEOPLE REFER TO HER AS THE "MOTHER OF THE NATION," SHE WAS NOT VERY INTERESTED IN COMPROMISE, OR IN A SLOW PATH TO EQUALITY. HER BELIEFS BECAME SO DIFFERENT FROM NELSON'S THAT THEY DIVORCED IN 1996.

Chapter 8
Free Mandela

The years at Robben Island never broke
Nelson's spirit. He never stopped believing that
South Africa could change. He exercised each
morning and read every evening. He studied law
through the mail. He learned Afrikaner history
and language. The darkest time for him in prison
was when he was forbidden to study. This lasted
four years. But Nelson was determined, and he
passed his intermediate law exams when he was
forty-five years old.

There was one joyful thing about prison life:
friendship. Prisoners were forbidden to talk, but
they found ways. They whispered as they worked
in the quarries and passed secret notes hidden
in the dirty dishes. They even organized work

slowdowns and went on hunger strikes. Mandela
might be in prison, but he was still a tree shaker!

Of all his friends in prison, Walter Sisulu was the person he relied on the most. Sisulu was Nelson's sounding board. He discussed all his ideas for achieving black equality with him. Mandela once said, "We walked side by side through the valley of death, nursing each other's bruises, holding each other up when our steps faltered."

Mandela also wrote a five-hundred-page autobiography on smuggled paper. He buried the pages, wrapped in plastic and hidden in cocoa containers, all over the prison courtyard. He encouraged other prisoners to study and learn, too. And although Nelson was a leader, younger prisoners were amazed at his humility.

Prison life was very difficult for Nelson. When illness prevented him from working in the quarry he was locked in a wet, cold, solitary cell apart from his friends. All he was given to eat was rice and water.

Meanwhile, Oliver Tambo was still traveling around the world telling everyone about Mandela and the fight against apartheid. He met with civil rights groups and government leaders. He set up international chapters of the ANC. World leaders who recognized him as the face of the new South Africa began to call for Mandela's release. Tambo also organized revolutionary fighters from training camps in nearby Tanzania and Zambia. He moved the fighters to Angola, on the border of a province controlled by South Africa. This sent a

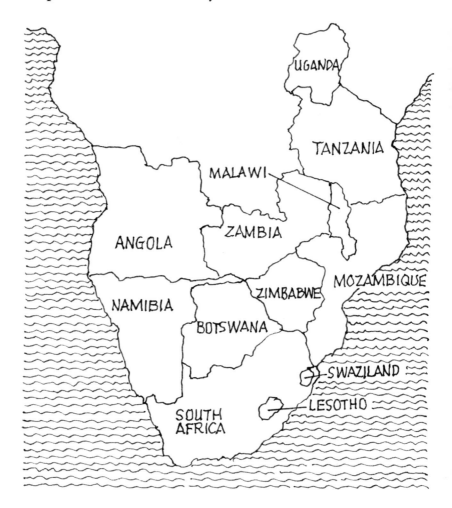

message to the white government of South Africa: The ANC was willing to go to war.

In 1976 the minister of prisoners offered to reduce Mandela's sentence if he would support the government's latest project, the Homeland System. They hoped to use Mandela's influence to support their own agenda. Mandela said no. The government tried to tempt him with better deals if he abandoned his friends. Again, Mandela said no.

Mandela was fifty-eight when the government passed a law declaring that all schools had to teach difficult subjects like math and science in the Afrikaans language. Most black children couldn't even understand Afrikaans, and had come to think of it as the language of their oppressors. So how did they have a chance of learning anything? Once again, the government was finding ways to further deny black students a decent education.

THE HOMELAND SYSTEM

IN 1970 THE SOUTH AFRICAN GOVERNMENT DIVIDED SOUTH AFRICA INTO SEPARATE STATES BY RACE. UNDER THE NEW ARRANGEMENT, CALLED THE HOMELAND SYSTEM, BLACK PEOPLE WOULD NO LONGER BE CITIZENS OF SOUTH AFRICA. THEY WOULD COME INTO SOUTH AFRICA ON TEMPORARY WORK PERMITS TO DO THEIR JOBS. BLACK PEOPLE WHO REFUSED TO LIVE IN THE HOMELAND ASSIGNED TO THEM—PLACES THEY HAD OFTEN NEVER EVEN BEEN TO BEFORE—WERE MOVED AGAINST THEIR WILL. BUT THESE "INDEPENDENT COUNTRIES" WOULD NEVER BE OFFICIALLY RECOGNIZED BY THE REST OF THE WORLD.

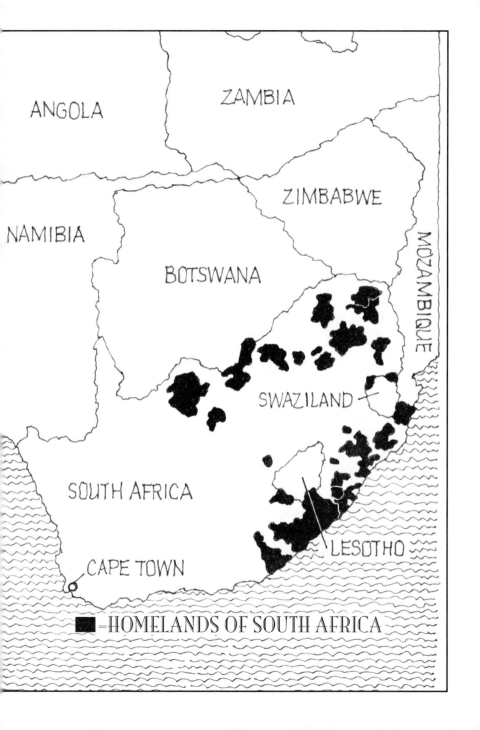

ANGOLA

ZAMBIA

NAMIBIA

ZIMBABWE

MOZAMBIQUE

BOTSWANA

SWAZILAND

SOUTH AFRICA

LESOTHO

CAPE TOWN

■=HOMELANDS OF SOUTH AFRICA

A group in the Soweto Township organized
a protest. Ten thousand students participated.
Some were only six years old. Yet the police

opened fire on them. The township of Soweto
became a battleground. Once again dead bodies
filled the streets, many of them children. Their

parents joined the fight. The fire of protest lit in
Soweto spread to other townships. The riots went
on for sixteen months before they were crushed.
Nearly one thousand people died and 5,980 were
arrested. The police did not lose a single man.

On Robben Island there were so many new prisoners that it was easier to keep everyone locked in their cells rather than make them work.

However, it did not matter how many civil-rights leaders were sent to

STEVE BIKO

prison. New leaders, such as Steve Biko, always came forward to take their place. Biko established a health clinic and community programs as well as classes in practical skills aimed at making black South Africans independent.

Steve Biko was arrested several times for his work. In 1977 he had been in police custody for twenty-five days when police announced he had died in his cell from going on a hunger strike. (A hunger strike is when someone refuses to eat to protest an injustice.) The truth was that Biko had been beaten and then left to die chained in his cell. No one was ever charged with his murder.

Police tried to prevent people from attending Steve Biko's funeral in King William's Town in Eastern Cape on September 25, 1977. But

twenty thousand black citizens and many white people, too, came to pay their respects. The United States and twelve other western countries sent representatives to attend. Protesters in other countries wanted their governments and other institutions to stop trade with South Africa.

The pressure on the white South Africans was mounting. Nelson Mandela was a symbol of hope for a better South Africa. He was the best known of all the activists. In 1980 the Johannesburg *Sunday Post*, a black newspaper, printed a petition to release him. The headline read: FREE MANDELA.

Would the government listen?

Chapter 9
State of Emergency

South Africa was going bankrupt, because so many foreign businesses would have nothing to do with the country. Riots broke out regularly. So the government made some changes. They desegregated public buses and theaters and gave some townships electricity. They let Indian and "colored" citizens elect people to represent them in the government—but not in the chamber of parliament that represented the white citizens. Many Afrikaner voters were angry at the changes, while many nonwhites didn't see much of a difference.

Nelson Mandela did see a difference in his own life. In April 1982, Mandela was moved to Pollsmoor prison near Cape Town. For the first

time in decades, he had a bed. Many believed
Mandela had been moved in order to separate
him from most of his Robben Island friends. This
way Mandela couldn't have as much influence,
couldn't cause as much trouble.

The president of South Africa said he was
willing to free Nelson if he came out against
violence as a way of ending apartheid. When
Mandela heard the offer he wrote out his answer
and gave it to his daughter Zindzi. She read it in a

crowded stadium in Soweto. It was the first time that Mandela's words had been heard legally in public since he'd been sent to prison.

Mandela wrote: "Only free men can negotiate; prisoners cannot enter into contracts. Your freedom and mine cannot be separated." Nelson would not accept freedom if it required him to support apartheid in any way.

In September 1989, fifty-three-year-old F. W. de Klerk was elected president of South Africa. Although he was a Nat Party leader, de Klerk had promised to negotiate with the ANC to solve South Africa's problems. De Klerk had Sisulu and others released from Robben Island. He had Mandela brought to meet with him in December. Two months later de Klerk announced the ANC was no longer an illegal group. Then he made an even bigger announcement: Nelson Mandela was going to be released from prison!

Chapter 10
President Mandela

On February 11, 1990, at 4:15 p.m., Nelson
Mandela stepped out of prison. He was seventy-
one years old, and had spent ten thousand days
behind bars. Outside Cape Town City Hall fifty

thousand people gathered to hear him speak. He chanted, *"Amandla!"* ("Power!") which meant "The power is ours!"

Older people hadn't seen Mandela in so long, they didn't know what to expect. Younger South Africans had never seen him. They expected an old man too tired to get involved in politics.

They were wrong. Freedom had recharged Mandela. He took a trip around the world where he was greeted with cheering crowds. In his

own country, he argued with many black South Africans who still did not want to work with white South Africans or hear about forgiveness. Violence had been part of their lives for so long, it seemed like the only answer. Nelson still believed that black people and white people should work together. He thought they could put their problems behind them.

White South Africans wanted Mandela to praise the government and be grateful for being let out of prison. Instead he encouraged foreign countries to keep refusing to trade with South Africa until apartheid was truly gone for good. He demanded nothing less than one person, one vote. He said, "When I was sent to prison twenty-seven years ago I had no vote . . . when I came out I still had no vote. That is due to the color of my skin."

President de Klerk dragged his feet when it came to real change. He may have been hoping that in time Mandela's influence would fade.

Black South Africans were frustrated at the lack of change. In August 1992 the ANC led a nationwide general strike, the largest in South Africa's history. In their demand to end apartheid, people all over the country refused to go to work. A month later in Bisho, South Africa, soldiers opened fire on an ANC rally, killing twenty-eight people and wounding almost two hundred more. On September 26, 1992, Mandela and de Klerk signed a Record of Understanding. It said that they would try to come to an agreement about the government. In 1993 Mandela and de Klerk were jointly awarded the Nobel Peace Prize.

NOBEL PEACE PRIZE

ALFRED NOBEL WAS A SWEDISH SCIENTIST AND THE INVENTOR OF DYNAMITE. HE ALSO MANUFACTURED WEAPONS. BUT AS HE GOT OLDER, HE DID NOT WANT TO BE REMEMBERED FOR DESTRUCTIVE THINGS. SO IN HIS WILL HE LEFT ENOUGH MONEY TO AWARD ANNUAL PRIZES FOR EXCELLENCE IN FIELDS THAT MAKE THE WORLD A BETTER PLACE. THE PRIZES ARE FOR ACHIEVEMENTS IN PHYSICS, CHEMISTRY, MEDICINE, AND LITERATURE. A FIFTH PRIZE IS ALSO GIVEN TO SOMEONE WHO WORKS HARD TO BRING ABOUT PEACE IN THE WORLD. IN TRYING TO BRING SOUTH AFRICA TOGETHER, MANDELA AND DE KLERK EARNED THAT HONOR.

The following year in April, South Africa held its first truly democratic election. The country would vote for representatives in the senate and the national assembly, as well as local governments in the provinces. Any of South Africa's over forty million citizens who were adults could vote, including black people. That meant millions of new voters. Nelson Mandela entered the race

for president. It's
hard to imagine
how exciting this
was for black South
Africans. When
candidate Mandela's
motorcade rolled
into a town people
rushed out
cheering. They
chanted his name,
danced in the
streets, and climbed
lampposts just to
get a glimpse of
their hero.

Of course
Nelson's friend
Walter Sisulu
helped in his

campaign for president. Sadly, Nelson's other closest friend, Oliver Tambo, did not live to see South Africa's first truly democratic election. He died of a stroke on April 24, 1993. Without all his work, Nelson might never have been released from prison.

Nelson ran for president against de Klerk. During the four days of the election people stood in line for hours to vote. When all the results were counted, the ANC had won 252 seats out of 400 in the National Assembly. That meant 252 black representatives in the national government. They also won sixty of ninety seats in the senate. De Klerk lost the presidency. As the runner-up he would serve as deputy president. He would be the

first white deputy president to serve under a black South African.

On May 10, 1994, Nelson Mandela became the first black president of South Africa.

Mandela served for five years. The people often called him "*Tata*," meaning "Father," or "Prisoner 46664" out of respect for his years at Robben Island. Mandela didn't have a lot of experience running a government, and South Africa's was more difficult than most. Even computer records for white citizens and black citizens were kept in two completely different databases on two

different computer systems. For once, Nelson did not have Walter Sisulu working by his side. His friend retired from politics after the election. He died in 2003.

South Africa's new constitution outlawed discrimination of all kinds. But many black South Africans still lived in poverty, and Nelson wanted to help them. He donated much of his salary as president to a fund for poor children. Even in his personal life Nelson was still making changes. On his eightieth birthday, he got married again, to Graça Machel, a children's rights activist, whom he had first met on a visit to Mozambique.

Mandela stepped down from the presidency in 1999. Nelson was replaced by Thabo Mbeki, followed by Kgalema Motlanthe and Jacob Zuma. All were black South Africans who were members of the ANC.

But Mandela's days of tree shaking were not over. He devoted himself to educating South Africans about AIDS. This cause was one that was very personal to him. His own son Makgatho died of the disease in 2005.

Nelson Mandela never stopped fighting for

South Africans. But he finally could enjoy time with his family. In 2010 he appeared at the World Cup soccer tournament, which South Africa hosted that year. It was the last time he appeared in public. He moved back to the village of his childhood where friends visited him often. Surrounded by his three remaining children, seventeen grandchildren, and a

growing number of great-grandchildren, with his wife by his side, Nelson Mandela looked out on a different South Africa. A South Africa that he helped create.

Nelson Mandela died on December 5, 2013, at his home in Houghton, Johannesburg, of complications related to a respiratory infection he suffered from in the last years of his life. People all over the world mourned Mandela and celebrated his legacy of peace and freedom.

TIMELINE OF
NELSON MANDELA'S LIFE

1918 — Nelson Mandela is born

1927 — Mandela's father dies and Mandela goes to live with Jongintal

1940 — Mandela is expelled from Fort Hare and flees to Johannesbur

1944 — Mandela joins the ANC and marries Evelyn Ntoko Mase

1948 — Apartheid begins

1952 — The ANC leads the Defiance Campaign
Mandela and Oliver Tambo open the first black law
partnership in the country

1956 — The Treason Trial begins

1958 — Mandela and Evelyn divorce
Mandela marries Nomzamo Winifred Madikizela

1960 — The Sharpeville Massacre occurs

1961 — The Spear of the Nation is founded

1964 — Mandela enters prison on Robben Island

1976 — Riots in Soweto occur

1977 — Steve Biko is murdered

1982 — Mandela is transferred to Pollsmoor Prison

1990 — Mandela is released from prison

1993 — Mandela and de Klerk win the Nobel Peace Prize

1994 — Mandela is elected president of South Africa

1996 — Mandela and Winnie divorce

1998 — Mandela marries Graça Machel

2005 — Mandela announces his son's death from AIDS

2013 — Mandela dies on December 5

TIMELINE OF
THE WORLD

The first European vessel, a Portuguese trading ship, sails around the Cape of Good Hope, South Africa	1488
The Boer War between the British and the Dutch ends	1902
Electric refrigerators for home use are invented	1913
World War I begins	1914
Women win the right the vote in the US	1920
Prohibition is repealed in the US	1933
Joseph Stalin dies	1953
The Berlin Wall is built	1961
The Smiley Face is invented Shakespeare's *Julius Caesar* is translated into Swahili	1963
Man lands on the moon	1969
Earthquake hits Lima, Peru	1974
Charles, the Prince of Wales, marries Lady Diana Spencer	1981
New Coke is invented and quickly disappears	1985
US passes anti-apartheid economic sanctions bill	1986
Pope John Paul II visits Cuba	1998
Barack Obama is reelected president of the US	2012

BIBLIOGRAPHY

*Denenberg, Barry. **Nelson Mandela: "No Easy Walk to Freedom,"** rev. ed. New York: Scholastic, 2005.

*Gaines, Ann Graham. **Nelson Mandela and Apartheid in World History**. Berkeley Heights, NJ: Enslow Publishers, 2001.

Irwin, Darrell D. "Awards for Suffering: The Nobel Peace Prize Recipients of South Africa." **Contemporary Justice Review**, June 2009.

Keller, Bill. "South Africa Unions Call General Strike." **New York Times**, July 2, 1992.

*Keller, Bill. **Tree Shaker: The Story of Nelson Mandela**. Boston: Kingfisher, Houghton Mifflin, 2008.

Maltz, Leora, ed. **Nelson Mandela**. Farmington Hills, MI: Greenhaven Press, 2004.

McKenzie Co. Public Library
112 2nd Ave. NE
Watford City, ND 58854
701-444-3785
librarian@co.mckenzie.nd.us

Mandela, Nelson. **Mandela: An Illustrated Autobiography**. Boston: Little Brown, 1996.

McSmith, Andy. "Oliver Tambo: The Exile." **The Independent**, October 15, 2007.

Nelson Mandela Centre of Memory website: **nelsonmandela.org**.

Nelson Mandela Foundation, ed. **A Prisoner in the Garden**. New York: Viking Studio, 2005.

Scott, Christina. **Nelson Mandela: A Force for Freedom**. New York: Random House, 2006.

* Books for young readers

105